UPRISING

Michele Battiste

UPRISING

Black
Lawrence
Press

Black
Lawrence
Press

www.blacklawrence.com

Executive Editor: Diane Goettel
Book and Cover Design: Amy Freels
Cover Art: "An enthusiastic insurgent recites Petöfi's 'Songs of Freedom' in
the broken shopwindow of the Soviet bookstore in Vaci utca," Autumn 1956,
Budapest, People's Republic of Hungary, © Erich Lessing

Black Lawrence Press
326 Bigham Street
Pittsburgh, PA 15211

Published 2014 by Black Lawrence Press.
Printed in the United States.

For
Erika Battiste Bedor

and in memory of
Joseph and Julia Nagy

Contents

Family Tree

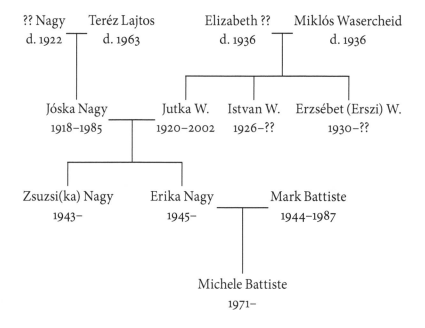

?? Nagy   Teréz Lajtos
d. 1922   d. 1963

Elizabeth ??   Miklós Wasercheid
d. 1936   d. 1936

Jóska Nagy   Jutka W.   Istvan W.   Erzsébet (Erszi) W.
1918–1985   1920–2002   1926–??   1930–??

Zsuzsi(ka) Nagy   Erika Nagy   Mark Battiste
1943–   1945–   1944–1987

Michele Battiste
1971–

Prologue, 2006

It should be the writer's prerogative
to tell the truth. To criticize anybody
and anything. To be sad. To be in
love. To think of death. Not to ponder
whether light and shadow are in
balance in his work.

—Gyula Háy, June 1956, Budapest

Learning the Dead Language

Forty-one letters in the alphabet—the longest *O* bending
my tongue back under itself, uncomfortable
as a cow in heat and just as graceful. Twenty years

since I mangled curses at the kitchen
table—*mokúska fasz, beszartam*
(squirrel dick, shit in my pants)—watching
color mottle her cheeks. He said *picsa*
meant pizza and waited for the scene
at lunch. She almost spit when I asked
for another piece of pussy, then turned
to smack her husband's back to keep
him from choking. I think I understood

once. Sounds drifting through
the house like kitchen smells, the way you know
the taste before you eat. But my English was their song
—a long, slow stroke across the violin's strings
and the *magyar* slept. After

the sermon, strange men resurrected a soldier's
song, hands on the casket, lowing in their throats.
My father said "too bad the old man never learned
English." I swore, mouthed "liar." My *nagypapa* and I

spoke. *Nagyon szép anyuka, drága kicsi nagymama,*
kit vagyok ma? A foreigner tripping
over unpronounceables and triple-placed suffixes, searching
for the language that will take my tongue
back, let me utter "this one" like Grandpa pointing
to a tool in the chicken shack, crouching at the belly
of his moonshine still. *Ez egy*, this one. *Ez egy*, pointing.
I reached, grabbed, felt the weight of it in my hands.

1. The Way to the Party

Arise *Magyar*, your country calls!
Now or never, our time compels!
Shall we be slaves? Shall we be free?
These are the questions. Answer me!
—**Sándor Petőfi, "National Song"**

Erika, November 29, 1944: The Russians are marching

and Budapest lives in sectioned-off coal cellars, black
   dust clogging the thin sieve of skin.
Evening swells, sirens beating on six inches of window
   like autumn breaking down on barren streets.
Jutka inhales on the decrescendo, the baby at her breast
   again, kicking her ribs—a soft metronome
   marking the rise and fall of mechanical howl,
   too slow for any melody but dirge and it is easy
   to forget that death is a mournful thing.

II

Night leans in, thick with shallow breathing
   of the building's remnants: nineteen
   in all and all but the babies
   balancing the edge of sleep.
Among the bodies Jóska creeps like a shade.

Jutka's lungs collapse with sigh. To cry would admit
   possibilities other than return, would tempt
   God to level this one reprieve with common
   tragedy, would wake the baby.

He whispers *wife*, a word he won't allow himself in hiding.
He whispers *the Russians are marching*, his fingers plying
   her waist. He reaches for his daughter, a burrowing creature
   cradled in her arms.
I won't raise a Ruszki bastard.

III

Jutka leads her husband to a corner, two walls at least
   and a headboard of rough brick.
Everyone pretends to sleep.

Jóska pretends his keening is a passion.
Jutka pretends nothing.
She is a clenched muscle, a heartbeat around her husband going
    soft inside her, finally asleep.

IV

Morning comes with gray street-level light silvering the window.
Jóska is gone, a kiss to her palm
    her skirt smoothed to her ankles.
Left behind: a sack of apples, bread, a snapped-neck chicken
    and my conception—a pre-emptive strike.

Jutka, January 4, 1945: Precautions

Erzsébet plump as a tree-ripened
peach, and the animals are starved.
I hide her in the closet, dress

her in three pairs of Jóska's trousers, smudge
her with sludge from the street. She heard stories

of other girls in their hands,
but understands them like a scary fairy tale,
like I understand the heaped

rubble of buildings, the body
of the locksmith in the doorway
of his store, boots and coat removed

as if by some loved one readying him
for much needed sleep.
Our mother would have placed

knives in our hands. Our papa
would have shipped us north, hidden
us in the woods like mules. I have

two watches and salami for barter,
Zsuzsika at my breast, my sister
clowning in men's clothes.

Jóska, March 3, 1945: Outlaw Dreams
of Budapest

Jutka, we have failed our mothers. Five hundred thousand have left
and these brittle streets are littered with strays. I can't tell friends
from invaders, everyone eyeing each other, blinking a code
of accusation and fear. When did our brothers start sucking
at Stalin's tit? We let them feed, grow fat, fall in love with their
nursemaid. I can see my ribs. Jutka, I am terrified of the prisons.
Inside, they smash violins, burn our paper, freeze men naked
in the basements. Jutka, I was such a bad soldier. Captured twice.
You'll laugh when I tell you stories of escapes, stupid Russians. But
I'm not clever. I hide. From here I see the Palace rubble, the Danube
flowing south like a coward and I envy it. Every bridge is ruined.
Jutka, my calendar has stopped. I wait for food, more news of you.
I hear a Captain took our building, now a Bolshevik headquarters.
You do their laundry, cook their dinner in the cellar. You are safe
and not starving. Jutka, I remember the cellar. Jutka, I hear you
are starting to show.

Jóska, March 14, 1945: Injury

Jutka, I miss your fingers, the touch I know only now that it's gone.
My fellow soldier is not deft, puncturing skin as he plies splinters
from my ass, the needle clumsy in his paws. His idea—a night out
of this hole, the danger receding. We disguised ourselves as ugly
spinsters, but Soviet dicks are incapable of better judgment than
their brains. Two repulsive specimens—carbuncles and stinking
beards—fancied our shapes, chased us laughing until our kerchiefs
flew, then ran like men hunting men. We ducked into a building
shredded by shells. From a window upstairs, a plank stretched
to the street. We slid bare-assed, skirts riding to our waists, yanked
the plank down in our wake. Their shouts were aimed better
than their bullets, and Jutka, that was my last escape. I wait
for the allies to take us and hope we serve better as pawns
than as carrion.

Jutka, April 2, 1945: Addressing the Captain

So you desert us. A new command, farther west.
Possible resistance, but what have your Reds left
standing? Imbeciles and ancients tottering

in the alleys, guts rotting from home
made brandy, a stench of wood smoke and spoiled
peach. Where are our men? 600,000 delivered

like freight to your liberation: a little
work in the Gulag. Go then.
With your restless fingers rubbing

your trigger, complaining of the taste
of our meat. Your soldiers are toothless
and grubbing, idiotic with guns and deliveries, barking

their ugly tongue. I asked one to put the perch
in the sink and he threw it in the toilet.
Erzsébet laughed and he slapped her, groped

her breasts. What a force you have
assembled! Bewildered by indoor plumbing
and girls. We are used

to men and you are only
what we are afraid of once
we get over our disgust.

Jutka, June 1, 1945: Train to Kecskemét

Even the river is begging.
The market is a barren whore.
Teréz, Jóska's mother, takes us

in. She once made dresses
from potato sacks,
but that was the other war.

The *pengő* is worthless, good for nothing
but wiping Zsuzsi's bottom. I leave her
with Erzsébet and onion-skin broth.

For trade, we packed towels, lace, my embroidered
bedsheets, edged in violets and poppies.
On the road to the station we talk

of pork and flour. Maybe butter, maybe
peppers, maybe eggs, noodles, a *gulyás*,
some cream. The lace is old but delicately

repaired, good enough for country
peasants who sweep their dirt floors into patterns,
desperate for a little nobility.

The train is filled: young Communists awkward
with privilege, pink-skinned and snuffling;
women with baskets like ours or more

precious, silver and candlesticks, porcelain jugs.
No space left but the roof and we climb.
Our bodies like thatch along the metal

slope, feet jammed against the risers
to hold us there, we revise. Maybe grain, lard,
a few pig's ears. The train lurches and the baby

lunges inside. Hand on my stomach,
I tell Teréz. Her mouth sets. "A traveler.
A gypsy. Not such a good sign."

Jutka, November 5, 1945: Free Elections

So the Smallholders won the government.
They haven't won the streets—a Ruszki pig
in every alley, rooting through dirty business.

Look at Jóska dancing in the garden with Erika, swinging
the infant as if she were made of ribbons.
The neighbors will think him drunk on *pálinka*, as if

anyone but Communists can get their hands
on even that rotgut. A good campaign, no?
A pig in every ally, a bottle of *pálinka* in every home.

Maybe I am bitter, as Jóska claims. He is
home, whole, Zsuzsika tripping his feet, Erika yawning
in his arms. And Erzsébet, home from school.

She is too old to hang on Jóska
like a child. I must tell her. Fourteen
and swelling. Trouble enough soon.

Jóska, February 12, 1946: The Republic of Hope

Land reform. Inflation stabilization. Socialist industry.
Collaboration with neighboring states. Already Nagy dismantles
the feudal system. To hell with the honorable barons and counts. Let
them heave spades, drive oxen, leave the people to their prosperity.
Jobs for everyone who wants to work, land for everyone who wants
to work it. For me, a promotion—head typesetter at the press.
England and France will look east for industrial advancement.
My daughters will wear smartly trimmed suits, travel west to teach
the latest technologies. So the Soviets still occupy the country.
The Americans are here, too. Allied interests in a burgeoning
democracy. Soon the treaty, and Hungary will be left to rise
once again from ash, the world's skeptic gaze astonished.

September 23, 1946: Reappearances

István, that worthless cur, fetid and drooling a stench of Soviet
vodka (vodka!) arrives half-dead on the doorstep, pockets empty
and good for nothing but scaring the neighbors. Jutka pets her
brother like a poodle and weeps over the bruises he no doubt earned
cheating a worker out of his pay. He'll have no piece of mine,
its worth a mystery. What democracy resurrects a monarch's
currency? Inflation isn't halted, it's disoriented. And somehow
a Communist's *forint* is worth more than mine; buying wine
and Austrian sweets for whores in fur-trimmed gloves and silk
stockings. I can't afford to feed another of Jutka's strays. Erzsi
is a peach, but István. No. I send him to my mother's, where he
must pay for his bed and noodles or he's out. My decision is made.
Jutka wrings her hands and stomps about.

March 18, 1947: This is Peace

Paris must rot the minds of diplomatic men—
rich cream sauces and the perfumed wrists
of dancing girls addling their brains.

How else could they leave us to the Ruszkis?
Not that the Western allies were anything
other than an audience for the show,

actors playing at democracy. Behind
the curtain, Soviets splice and knot, tangle
and cut until only their puppets are left

on stage, mouthing multi-party lines.
The treaty is signed. Western forces applaud
and rush the exits before the final curtain.

June 15, 1947: Slicing up Parties like Salami

Bewildering, this Hungarian democracy—leftist Smallholders plot
with Communists to toss the leaders out and the right wing itches
to use majority clout to decree a homogenous government.
The Soviets claim conspiracy, exile Ferenc Nagy, vanish Kóvacs
somewhere in Siberia. Who wins? The left-wing is deluded if they
don't think their leaders aren't next to disappear. The Communists
drop other parties' members in their pockets, place Muscovite
darlings in key positions. And the Soviets nod "yes, yes, yes."
The West could stop them, but the West is too busy with its love
for Austria and other "victims" of the war.

August 31, 1947: Free Elections, Part II

Such persuasive campaigning at the polls.
The astute insights, the crafted arguments,
the difficult questions engaging open minds.

What would you call such a convincing
approach? Rifle butt rhetoric? Nose breaking
analysis? I can't discuss political

strategies right now—Jóska wasn't swayed
and now I've got a bloody mess of a Smallholder
husband, two shrieking children, and Erzsébet

so rattled she can barely steady the compress
on Jóska's crown, his hands on her waist
to keep her from shaking. I will quickly predict,

however, a slim Communist victory, considering
their corrective method of replacing faulty
ballots with acceptable ones.

January, 1948: Jóska Commiserates on the Corner

My printing press has been declared too valuable for anyone
but a loyal Communist, so now I shiver in the factory shipyard,
my salary halved, drilling sheet metal to the skeleton of a hull. Jutka
works a shift at the steel factory, her palms flecked gray with metal
filings. They heal stinging. Her pay buys milk and flour, some
peppers and lard, nothing more. And nothing stays—an assembly
line straight to Moscow while our store fronts distend like empty
bellies. Three hundred million American dollars in reparations,
but we can't count machinery they looted after the war. We can't
count 200,000 men swallowed by the Gulag. Did I tell you they shot
at me as I crept to a ditch to fill my helmet with water? The war was
three days over. They are greedy for everything, even my flinching.
Today, Jutka brought Erika to a People's Nursery. It was dark.
She was late for her shift. What could she do but leave Erika sleeping
in the hallway, hope the republic rouses itself before our youngest
lunges from her dreams.

August 4, 1948: A Paper for the People

The presses shut down, editors denounced
for political unreliability or threatened
with arrest. Some limped along, sneaking

in a sliver of news between profiles of model
comrades and exaltations of Stalinist success.
Writers are condemned as reactionaries,

fired as liabilities, working now in brick
factories or worse. We are left with hacks
and *Szabad Nép*, its veil of pulp

and smeared ink obscuring the world
beyond East Berlin. Every worker forced
to subscribe or face arrest, and stories

of the ÁVH basements keep us in line.
Jóska leveled his pride and applied for a red
Party card. He was denied for western

sympathies. I guess they mean his faith
in a multi-party system, which he renounced
after they broke his teeth at the last election.

December 24, 1948: A Socialist Christmas

Ever since my scandal with Father Álmos at 19
(his sleepy eyes as sweet as poppy paste), I've not been
much for the Church. Yet I believe the devil

will torch the asses of the Reds who tossed Mindszenty
in jail. What holiday is this, the Cardinal a traitor
to the people, the people too frightened to light up

their trees? I'll be damned if I waste weeks
of hoarding—we *will* feast: a duck and blood
sausage, *paprikás* potatoes, red cabbage

with vinegar, sugar, and caraway seeds, butter
for bread, pickled cucumbers and beets, a small
bottle of plum *pálinka* for Jóska and István,

and chocolate cake with real cream! Teréz
brought her silver plate, Erzsi and the girls decorate
the tree with bits of tin and winter berries. Tonight

our windows will be well-lit and steamy. Tomorrow
we will wake with hefty bellies, worry later
about what any informant may have seen.

May 15, 1949: Free Elections, Part III

A single slate—the Populist Front—made up of Communists
and sycophants. Why bother to vote? But everyone does, wary
of the consequences a lack of enthusiasm can provoke. Jutka drags
even worthless István to the polls. The girls skip along with my
mother. A loyal family on display.

Erika, August 24, 1949: The Age of Reason Arrives Early in a Socialist Society

My birthday. A cake and four candles
but no cream. A chocolate bar for me only.
Zsuzsi's sad. I give her a square. She takes
another when I dance with Daddy. It's okay.
Everyone is here. Mama, Daddy, Zsuzsi, Erzsi,
Grandma, Uncle István.
I got a new dress for my dolly.
Then we sing but next door is noisy. Banging,
shouting, crying. But the Dobós are always quiet.
They give me cookies.
Bang Bang Bang on our door and the party stops.
Three men frowning. One comes in stomp
stomp stomp. Looks at my chocolate.
Mama says, "the baby's birthday." He stomps
into the kitchen, comes out with Daddy's salami.
I see the Dobós in the hallway with suitcases.
Mrs. Dobó cries and Mr. Dobó has a purple cheek.
The man shouts at Daddy, "Papers!"
Then they leave, pulling on Mrs. Dobó
like she is a dog on a leash.
Erzsi takes me and Zsuzsi in the garden and we play.
I say the men are bad and ugly. Erzsi says
hush and no one speaks. I know this
secret. Not the first one I keep.

October 8, 1949: The People's Prosperity

Perilous, the high-ranking jobs of government. Nagy
transformed to pariah. Rajk tortured, puppet-tried and hanged.
His cabinet and cronies lucky to be only purged

from the Party. Only Rákosi is safe, Stalin's best student.
Who goes and who stays is anyone's guess.
It's best to be quiet, poor, have nothing.

The new neighbors, named Horváth, carry
membership cards. They brought a piano, the smell
of eggs frying. I don't begrudge them their

breakfast—the ÁVH has stopped lurking on our street.
The husband knows István, smiles like a little
boy when I mention his name, and flirts

like gypsy with Erzsébet, sneaks her candies
when the wife is busy cutting black market
meat in the kitchen. Yesterday on line at the butchers

we were taunted by Soviet soldiers clutching
their crotches and calling out that they had the meat
we need. A woman in front of me threw

a stone. The men hooted and called
the police. She was arrested. I was happy
to have her place.

March 4, 1950: Good Luck in the Labor Kitchens

My daughters' eyes brim with the freeze
of a long winter and one scrawny row
of grocer's stock. Lines everywhere promise

frostbitten toes and empty baskets, our factories
churning out munitions instead of lamps
or chocolate, our small stores

of jams and herring and beans filling
Russia's pantries. Too frequently the girls follow
me to the labor kitchen, warm their noses

over thin soup. And I am lucky.
To be here, to have them with me.
Cica Hubay, the professor's wife

who once bought Teréz's lace for the hem
of her petticoats, was held at the hospital until
the twins were born. Her husband already deported

to the Csongrád *kolkhosz,* she had two
months with the babies before she was forced
to join her husband and surrender her sons to the state.

Erika, July 30, 1950: Family Life

Work makes Daddy sad. He builds big ships
    that go nowhere. His bosses are ugly, their tongues
    twisting up words like tree roots. They shout
    Russian sounds that mean *stupid* and *slow.*
When Daddy comes home, his face is twisted
    like a Russian tongue.
He shouts at everyone, especially István who smells
    like rotten peach and sleeps in Daddy's chair after eating
    more bread than anyone.
I cheer Daddy up with Zsuzsi. We sing songs
    we made up about a fox in the garden. Erzsi
    dances through the room, pokes Daddy
    in the arms and belly when she passes.
Then he smiles.

November 25, 1950: Ganz Factory Shipyards

Twenty ships since the war, all sailing east. Soviets bleeding us like livestock before the butchering. We give them skin and meat and muscle and they want more—5-year plans, 200% increased production. But they've looted our parts and pieces, every bolt and screw in short supply. So we substitute a nut here, a gear there. Ships return to the yard in a month, and the stinking Ruszkies claim sabotage. You want a Russian case of sabotage? An Újpest Factory worker arrested because his machine couldn't stand the strain of shitty Soviet cotton. We get "voluntary" overtime, peace loan deductions, mandatory meetings before clocking in and *Szabad Nép* discussions every night. Holidays, workers "spontaneously" honor Stalin with our services. It's a wonder no one has indulged in actual sabotage, did a little this or that, watch a ship sink before it even reaches the bend at Vasúti Bridge. But you never heard me say it.

2. Budapest Voices, 1951

*Between the summers of 1950 and 1951,
the period considered to be the height
of Rákosi's Terror, 70,000 Hungarians
were deported to USSR, most likely
to work camps in Siberia, and 80,000
were deported to collective farms
(kolkhoszek) or forced labor camps
in Hungary's most rural areas.*

Judit Fekete

I'll not call it a vocation or skill, rather,
a pious countenance, a disappearing
face. The spies of the ÁVH aren't difficult
to spot—better shoes and more often drunk,
blacking out their guilt. A name and nod to one
person passing on the corner, and all that is needed
is known. So far this week: Robert Turani,
assembly leader at Standard Factory;
Dr. Bizza Piroska at Rókus Kórház hospital;
Mr. and Mrs. Gyula Fehér, proprietors of the Jókai
coffee house.

Nancy Gross, an apple-cheeked mother
on Akácfa Street, monitors the movements
of all high officials. Ajtony Attila, an ambitious
young man, befriends youth in good families, tricks
them into professing western sympathies.
When not working, he meanders through libraries,
noting the names of children reading
literature of the West.

Éva Király

Typist, Ministry of the Interior

A list of persons deported today:

- Baroness Jenöke Forster, widow, age 74, retired owner of the Ace of Spades bar. Not a member of any political party, led a retiring life.

- Dr. Tamas Benelek, lawyer, age 38, deported to Tiszasöly with his British wife and three children. Slated for heavy labor at a shipping agency.

- Col. Tersanszky, trucker, age 51, with his Danish wife. Present at Benelek's home when the ÁVH arrived.

Miksa Beckmann

When the Arrow Cross came in '44, I was wily, one
step ahead and always hiding. I knew the ghetto,
its shadows and recesses, the corners
that transformed a body into stone or a stick
of furniture. I lost my children to foresight
in '36. My husband, faithful to Hungary, let them leave
us behind. I lost him to Auschwitz. He was not
as stealthy. All I had left was my life and I hung

on to it. I should not have become complacent, believing
the Stalinist dream, growing light and large
with greedy breathing, deluded to think the air
free. Once again my life is contained in a suitcase,
25 kilos and 60 years of suffering.
They are deporting me to the village of Jaszapati
because of a suspicious foreign contact—
my daughter, Vera Beckmann, residing at
1029 Central Avenue, Ocean City, New Jersey.

Gabor Csáki

It was an honor to serve
the Hungarian Peasant Delegation
at the Agricultural Conference in Moscow.
I described the extravagant success
of industrialized farming on the transdanubian
plains, testimony to Stalin's genius.
The other delegates nodded, unsurprised,
my argument evident in the city's
shops. In every store sits mountains
of butter marked "Hungarian Surplus."
I walked the markets of Moscow with pride,
but wished I could have a little to take home.
No butter in Hungary to stretch
our rations of bread, not even on the black market.
So I hear.

Jenö Korpas

12th District Chairman, Agricultural Council

Twenty-four tons of cucumbers, destined
for the canning plant, delivered
to a hog-fattening pen. By the time the mistake
was discovered, the cucumbers vanished
and the shipping crates were firewood. Sabotage
will be the cause. There will be arrests,
interrogations. Traitors will be rooted
out—those who stole the vegetables
and the provocateurs insinuating
that Party members made black market
capitalist gains. Only one signature on
the shipping papers, mine, and no one
can deny my loyalty.

Pál Kása

Geza Hánák bet me two pounds
of blood sausage that I could not prove
Rákosi himself predicted his own downfall.
Now I sit in a dark basement cell
of headquarters awaiting another
round of questioning, my left eye
swollen shut. The violation:
requesting an 18-month old
copy of *Szabad Nép*. In its pages,
a transcript of a a Rákosi speech stating,
"If bread rationing were introduced
in Hungary again, that would mean
the end of the regime." When I get
out of here, Hánák better have
those sausages wrapped in a bow.

Ildi Kis

My nightdress worn to a washrag, I went
shopping. Four stores boasted
nightwear in their windows, but nothing
inside except clerks afraid
to sell items on display. I resorted
to a People's Store and its one
rough pair of men's pajamas, so badly
cut I could grow another ass and not rend
a seam.

"How extraordinary," I said, "that in our
seventh year of progressive socialism,
no new nightwear can be purchased."

A woman wearing a Party badge popped out
from behind a rack. "Comrade, you can't
find a nightdress because the people
are now so enormously rich. They buy
in such quantities, production can't keep up."

Not wanting to wear my new pajamas
in jail, I kept my mouth shut.

Tibor Weiss

Mortician, Rókus Kórház Hospital

Expelled persons who committed suicide this week:

- Peter Kozmai, Professor of English, French and German, age 45—unidentified poison

- Endre Morvay, Carpet Merchant, age 52, and his wife—veranol. (The wife was saved and deported to Nyirseg)

- Béla Somogyi, Banker, age 50—evisceration

- Dr. Tibor Fekete, Lawyer, age 39—opened gas valves in his apartment

- Arpad Kaszas, Band Leader, age 45—jumped from the 3rd floor window.

János Gáspár

I murdered a man in Romania, fled
to Hungary and joined the Communists.
They were happy to have me.
A country practiced at the art
of reinvention is sympathetic
to a man with my recent turn
of fortune. Perhaps we help
each other rise from the ash of a past
most profitable to forget. Have you seen
the new Persian rugs in my flat? The closet
full of finely-threaded suits? I work
for rewards, a job many would not dirty
their hands with.

I find out who has money to spend, invite
them to a club, order the bottles, then direct
the fine women who work for me.
Dancing evolves into sex, sex into an orgy. Who
can resist? I report this and other indiscretions
to the ÁVH, privately blackmail as compensation
for my troubles. Don't think my life
is without care or worry. The ÁVH,
in turn, blackmails me and threatens
to turn me over to the Romanians,
which would mean my death.

Father Pál Ormos

The sign nailed to the church
door reads *Closed for the lack of God.*
Angelic young matrons visit
the old priests, say they'll take them
to the hospital, and deliver them
to jail. We're not permitted
inside hospitals, the dying denied
last rites, their rosaries swapped
out for pictures of Stalin. Christmas
is now Feast of the Pine Tree,
and the birth we celebrate is baby
Josef's. The three wise men have been replaced
by three jackasses who know to keep
quiet. God said, "Thou shalt not
worship false idols before me." God has said
a lot of things.

András Bak

I thought my store safe, the stock
a humble pile of rugs, my son the only
employee. But the Party has one hundred eyes
of Argus for any *forint* not falling
into their pockets. So deportees sell their carpets
when forced from their homes. So the Party
nationalizes the carpet business.

I had half a million *forint* in merchandise
when the police arrived. They grabbed
the thousand in my wallet and fined me 15,000
for "irregular" accounts. It equaled everything
in my cashbox. Penniless, I was warned
not to talk, as if anything was left that silence
could protect.

Zsuzsa Horváth

Most thought the safest place
was behind the red skirts of the Party—
always a salary, always a little meat,
the ÁVH on our side. But that kind
joined for their own benefit, kindled
a little conviction to save their
skin.

In September, all state employees
must write a new confession
under supervision, not knowing
there will be oral exams in the spring.
Any difference between the two
is grounds for expulsion.

Kalmán Sopron

Before the liberation, I had no world
beyond the *puszta,* the four room cottage
shared with the Nagys and the Haazs, our sty kept
beneath the window so our ears could keep
watch of the livestock in our sleep.

Now, like many of my comrades who grew
to know a peasant's place, I hold
a new position, one much more suited
to my untapped intelligence and guile.

I attend university, raise my status as I raise
my voice at Party meetings, discern
informants and chew their
ears with rabid convictions
and contempt for the church.

To reward my zeal, recruiters
from the Soviet Russian Institute
"suggested" I apply for admittance.
It seems candidates have fallen off,
a consequence of the many scholarships
to the USSR of indefinite length.

It is a distinction, I am told,
that I cannot refuse.

Cica Hubay

This is life after deportation. We walk,
forbidden to ride carts, forbidden
to enter the market before 11:30, when
everything has been snatched up.
Forbidden to have money, forbidden
to travel more than a stone's throw
from our *kolkhosz*. Any farmer caught
helping us is condemned as an enemy
of the people.

When my mother came, the village
council threatened to deport her. Her crime—
visiting the people's enemy when she could be
working for the Republic.

We trade clothes for food, labor all day
for two *forint*. The lowliest Party typist
makes 40 *forint* a day. I used to host luncheons
for Westerners attending my husband's lectures.
I took their wives for coffee and chestnut creams
along the Danube. Now any barefoot urchin
can denounce me for a few hundred *forint*
and a chicken in the pot.

They have taken my sons. Today they ask
for the voluntary contribution
of our wedding bands for the glory
of the State.

György Deák

A comrade's duty, to educate the proletariat,
to privilege workers whose backs are straining
beneath construction of the Republic. I am a poor
man, too. A lowly manager of a milk
shop. Every day is hardship, stretching
my meager stock, resisting bribes and other
ÁVH traps, limiting even nursing mothers
to half rations.

The crone was so ancient I almost
mistook her for a pile of twigs.
I thought it made sense, giving
her sugar or soap instead, insisting
every drip of milk is needed
for workers. Is it too much to expect a small
and reasonable sacrifice for the good
of Hungary? She attacked me
with the strength of a rabid
dog, and the police were called
to pull her off and remove her
from the premises.

Zsigmond Lajtha

It is best for everyone, the mothers,
their brats. The state will churn
out reliable workers instead of sticky urchins.
Magda Bódy lives apart from her husband,
an untrustworthy sod working the mines
near Romhany. Her son, age four, attends
the local kindergarten.

My strategy—an invitation
to a children's medical exam.
When the women arrive, I explain
the town's obligation to supply
500 women volunteers
for a traveling labor brigade.
To alleviate their burdens, each mother
is asked to voluntarily entrust
her child to the state.

Some mothers cry, beg, sink
to the floor. Bódy was easy, fainting dead
away. I am not a heartless man. When she woke,
I spent valuable time explaining the benefits
extended to her son as a ward of the state.
I gave her 3,000 forint, 300 more than the official
allotment, because she is meek and lovely,
and it can be difficult for a mother to lose
her child.

3. Steam in the Pot

Till now we have been abject slaves,
Shaming our forebears in their graves;
Those who so freely lived and died
Can find no rest in sullied ground.
—Sándor Petőfi, "National Song"

Jutka, April 1, 1952: Family of the Accused

Sixteen months since the ÁVH took
Jóska, called him mastermind, spit
the word sabotage. I heard nothing

for weeks, sent István to his connections,
hoping for news. He came home, cautioned
to stop digging in dog shit, or he'll start

smelling like the one who made the mess.
The black coats came anyway, cruising
the boulevards in their black car before taking

me to Headquarters. Terror House.
They said Jóska confessed. They read
"sentenced to six years for a plot to destroy

property of the Republic." My turn.
Nine hours of questioning, no break, no water,
no toilet. Threatened with prison, the loss

of my daughters. A few slaps from a fat
hand with a heavy ring, then let go.
Neighbors avoid me, afraid my blight

is catching. Comrades at the factory monitor
my attendance at education meetings, to whom
I speak, my levels of production. My pay is docked

for inefficiency. I received four words from Jóska
through the wife of a friend of an ex-inmate
of Sátoraljaújhely prison. She bumped into Erzsi

at market, dropped the note in her basket.
I'll be home soon in his hand. It's not fair
to Erzsi. At 21, she should be courting,

dreaming of a wedding night. Instead
she stands beside me on the assembly line,
turning gray with metal dust.

July 12, 1952: Waiting

On nights the girls sleep deeply, I risk
Western radio, ghosted voices
whispering their enchantments.

If they woke, Zsuzsi would keep
quiet, but Erika could slip, or worse,
denounce me. A good little Pioneer,

on guard against any whiff of Western influence.
But better for us that she's a model Communist,
not spitting Jóska's anti-Party drivel. The radio

sustains my neighbors, rallying them to resist,
teasing with hints of assistance when the time
comes. The men listen for clues to know

how and when the revolution will begin,
as if the U.S. is itching to liberate
us. That nonsense is no comfort to me.

I tune it to the gypsy music, prohibited
under the regime, and remember
how Jóska danced with me, then

Erzsi, then the girls, each clutching
a leg, Zsuzsi on one foot, Erika the other,
lifted by their father's steps.

Jóska, August 23, 1952: The Political Prisoner

I. 60 Andrassy Street, Budapest

I lasted eighteen days at the house of terror—skintight cells,
infested, dank with water. A board and a bucket. They kept me
up for days, then a blanket of darkness until I knew the world
ended without me. Brick walls do not block out screams, and I
had my share of activities. They said my shoes needed resoling,
tipped back the chair I was tied to, beat my soles with rubbers
sticks until I fainted. I couldn't remove my shoes for two days.
Baths of ice up to the waist, while lamps burned my skull
and back. The dentist came. I felt the drill skip and choose
its spot, bore into enamel, the nerve left exposed. A sip of water
made me bawl. They broke me administratively—threatened
to send my file to the bottom of the pile where it would not
surface for four months. I knew a man who'd been in for two.
A skeleton in shoes. I signed their papers, was tried and
transferred to Sátoraljaújhely, never once thinking of Jutka,
Zsuzsi, Erika. I was a ghost.

II. Sátoraljaújhely Prison

But a ghost could never stink so much. We've 24 cells built
for 60. The commander kept double that until the Justice
Ministry's inspection deemed the facility underutilized. They
shipped men until cinderblocks bulged like a Muscovite's belly.
Only a few here are criminals, bribed by the guards to spy on
politicals. The commander locks men in dark cells for invisible
offenses. Still, we get bread, black coffee, beetroot soup at noon
and six. Sometimes a little meat. And the real insurgents whisper
promises of a western liberation soon. But every day ends
in night, and every night is unending. Everywhere I turn, backs
hunched, quivering in sleep.

Erika, September 9, 1952: A Young Pioneer

Mama says what they say
about Daddy isn't true, but when Comrade Teacher
pulled me off Dani Tóth, my knees pinning
his chest like Zsuzsi taught me, Old Fenyő said
she'd talk to Mama about *my* wretchedness.
I thought I'd get the switch. When Mama left
the classroom with her angry cheeks and proud
walk, I knew my bottom was saved.
Home, she pulled me and Zsuzsi close,
said Daddy was an enemy
of the state and the People's
Revolution. Her lips thinned
to worms squirming on a hook.
Mama said we must pretend it's true
or we'll be enemies of the People, too,
and then the People will take us away.
After Mama sleeps, Zsuzsi and I
whisper about what to do.
The Pioneers say report our parents
if they ask us to lie or if they hide
money or paper or food.
Zsuzsi says don't be stupid or I'll cream you
and cut off your braids. The Pioneers
are the People.
Are we the People, too? I ask.
The real people, she says, and rolls
her back to me.
There's a difference, I guess.
Tomorrow, when I apologize to Dani Tóth
in front of the whole class, my lips
will squirm like worms, and mama
didn't have to ask for that.

October 12, 1952: Homecoming

He came back like they do
in the movies—a shadow
on the doorstep on a moonless

night, his hat pulled low,
his shoulders hunched
to the rain. Everyone says

they return to their selves,
week by week, like the fat
coming back to their bellies,

like the friends who arrive,
finally, with gifts of soured
cream or cherry jam, as if

our whole family had been
away and sorely missed. Nights
are better, the bed coaxing

him to sleep, his body settling
into me as if it knows, before the man
can believe, he is home.

November 26, 1952: Homecoming, II

Returned, but not yet home. Not that I have the luxury to linger
in the past, mope over my fate. But how does a man come home
if not from a day's work, sink a sore body into a chair, his daughters
making a game of unknotting his boots. The official lists of workers
include scores on political attitude, reliability, past activities, Party
status—everything but the size of the cock we must suck to keep
our jobs. The boss at the steel factory suggested I go west to
the mines where I can break what's left of my back for 600 forint
a month. "Jutka," I say, "we must find a way out." She covers
her head with her apron. Talk like that, she says, will see my ass
back in jail.

December 14, 1952: In the Cupboard

Uncle István ate the egg again
Mama's hands already a mess
    of flour and fat when she found the shell pretending
    to be full, a hole chipped in its bottom
It's the drink that makes him do it
Mama scolding, "sucking at your *pálinka* like a baby
    at its bottle"
But babies don't eat Sunday soup
    noodles floating on the surface, hiding
    treasure: cracked bones to be fished out and pried open
Papa drags István off the couch, calls him
    ragged cat's cunt as he kicks his bottom
"Look at your nieces," mama screams
    but Zsuzsi and I hide under the table, hold
    on to each other's sleeves
Noodles without egg sink to the bottom of the pot
    and burn easy
They sink in my stomach like ashes glued to an anchor
No fishing. A dead pond.

After István runs, papa pulls us up and tucks us
    in the bedcovers with mama waving her sticky hands,
    tells us stories of a country with eggs and potatoes
    and sausage for every breakfast
But I want what István wanted: thin-skinned yolk
    breaking like hunger breaks, a memory of so many eggs
    one missing won't matter
"István," papa says, "will bring back an egg."
Zsuzsi and I lick mama's fingers still, wait for István
    to come home.

March 5, 1953: The Death of Stalin

The last line of the last verse of the last book. The End. While
the nation passes itself off as mourning, Muscovites scramble
for seats of power (or to save their own asses, no difference). Rákosi
must be shitting his pants, a puppet without a hand, and no telling
who will now pull the strings. It is perilous to hope for change,
but everyone indulges. The workers are in the last stages of distress.
No matter if you are a *Stakhanovite* or, like me, a wiper of toilets
at the Radio Factory, you can do the math:
> nine hours of labor + one morning hour
> of patriotic songs + one evening hour
> of *Szabad Nép* review = eight hours
> pay, − 18% for inefficiency − voluntary
> peace loan contributions.
No one has money to demand the consumer goods that no one
is producing, despite the production goals that no one can fulfill.
The boss is comfortable, always American cigarettes and nylons
for his wife. And we cling to the jobs, terrified that our neighbor
on the line takes a note every time we roll our eyes. Hungary is a pot
full of steam, the lid about to blow. Stalin's pyre thickens the heat.

June 16, 1953: The Death of Stalinism

The Soviet Central Committee condemns Stalinism and the past
actions of Hungarian Communists—a whole herd summoned
to Moscow, a trip often traveled in one direction. No longer just
workers talking about U.S. intervention. Like an Arrow Crosser
shucking his green coat for a red card after the war, the boss
already brags, "I'll get a good job in an allied occupation, become
the favorite of American whores."

July 20, 1953: High Hopes

Again Jóska's gone missing. Off drinking
I bet, dreaming with István like two teenagers:
real socialism, amnesty for politicals, abolition

of internment camps. I hope, too. Maybe Jóska
can work as a printer again, stop talking about
a border crossing. No telling when he'll cross

paths with an agent provocateur.
They are swarming. Yesterday a woman
taken to Terror House for showing

a friend a letter from the West.
A fidgety character loitered at our stoop,
hinted at Jóska's third cousin

in Sweden, offered to arrange passports
for 2,000 *forint* each. We weren't fooled,
but their entrapments bewitch. And now

Teréz is looking for Erzabet to help
with laundry. Another one missing. Maybe a suitor,
finally. Maybe a state clerk with a Party salary.

June 17, 1954: Erika's Young Pioneer Report on Nagy's Policies

Imre Nagy, the father of agricultural reform, rid our land of aristocratic pestilence and the neo-feudal oppression that lasted through the war. As leader of Hungary, he corrected Rákosi's harsh policies that were an unfortunate result of his brutally enforced cult of personality. Many innocent men have been released from prison. Increased resources have been allocated to agricultural development and the production of consumer goods. Industrial norms have been eased. Communal farms can be dissolved if the majority of members choose to do so. Deportees are allowed to return to their homes in Budapest. These gentler policies are welcomed by the workers, who discuss daily their effect on the people's progress.

(But when the Dobos came back,
    the Horváths left them standing
    in the hallway with their broken suitcase.
I watched as Mrs. Horváth handed out
    Mrs. Dobo's mother's teapot,
    the orange-flowered one she filled
    with lemonade for me.
Mrs. Horváth said there's nothing
    left. The ÁVH took everything.
    Then she cried.
"What can we do," she shouted.
    "This is our home."
Even the hallway dust was silent
    as the Dobos crept like turtles away.)

October 10, 1954: Intervention and Self-Interest

The newsmen's mouths foam as they shout down Nagy's reforms. Moscow is the rabid dog biting their ankles, growling to rein Nagy in. So they ratify, black out the small glimpses of sky beyond the curtain. Neighbors prowl the bars, cry "why, why" into their swill. It's the Russian belly and Communist vault, filled with Hungary's mangled fingers and broken backs. Our lamp factories turn out flame throwers, our chocolate factories mold machine guns. *Tokaji* flows to the heart of Moscow and Hungary is weak from the loss of blood. Two hundred tons of butter scent the countryside, warming in boxcars headed east, east, east. Our agriculturalists forced to factory jobs, leaving our farms in the hands of idiots. This summer, schoolchildren working the beet fields of Veszprém stripped acres of roots and tended the weeds. The peasants don't bother to produce a stalk of wheat, an ear of corn; their stores emptied before the first loaf of bread rises. Did we really think the Soviets would surrender their bread basket? Instead, they pat our heads and congratulate us on the fine quality of flannel nightshirts we produce for trade with the West. And the West won't shut up about revolution.

January 5, 1955: Fidelity

Twenty-two and a one-half months—six hundred
eighty one days—I waited, faithful, heartsick,
frozen between dread and hope. All that time he dreamt

of coming home to the little whore. That viper
in my nest. A dozen admirers with a dozen beds,
but she spread her legs in mine. Not enough

to steal some other woman's man, she robbed
her own sister! But he is no treasure, no better
than a witless mutt that won't stop licking

its own dick. Teréz begs me to take him
back, to think of the girls, to recognize a man
for a man. If that's the measure of a man,

then I'm done with them. I'm done with sisters,
too. The Soviets don't need bother breaking
us. We do it ourselves.

February 11, 1955: A Small Indiscretion

Jutka, my flower, my blood and bread, my life, I am once again held captive. The streets between my mother's home and ours are prison bars. You should see the wasted mess I am without you, all tics and tremors. The nightmares return, but this time, you are the warden, kicking me while the girls look on. Times are worsening, Jutka. You must let me come home. Russia's regime changes once more, and Nagy is in disfavor. You know what happens to fatherless children when the Party cracks down. And I love only you. Do you not ache for me as I ache to see your smile, to feel your nimble fingers straighten my collar, to hear you scold me for spoiling the girls? I cannot think of your neck or thigh without breaking down. It was meaningless, drunken, a small indiscretion I regret. Jutka, I hear you are recovered, laughing in cafes with girls from work. Jutka, I am at your knees.

June 22, 1955: Homecoming, Part III

We are a family like the last time
    we weren't then were. Daddy here
    then gone. Then here.
Four bodies walk room to room like ghosts hoping
    to be left alone, making other bodies
    nervous.
Erzsébet has not come home and Mama says
    its time for her to find a husband, make
    her own family.
Daddy and Mama are careful, as if each
    is a body made of glass. Zsuzsi says
    stay out of their way.
But they aren't yelling or quick with a slap,
    just sad, and Daddy mutters to his hands,
    "It takes time."
They talk at dinner of the politics
    we celebrate at school—Nagy stepping
    down, his New Course denounced
    as rightist, Rákosi repairing
    the damage, Hungary a world
    power, part of the Warsaw Pact.
Krushchev is like a fickle schoolmate,
    making friends with Tito and saying
    nasty things of Stalin.
But Mama and Daddy stare at the table
    and chew slowly, their secrets getting
    in the way of everything.

December 31, 1955: Small Steps

Inch by inch, we take our discontent beyond the guarded whispers
at doorways to the streets. Shiftless writers are good for something
other than filling cafes with smoke and speeches: a letter to
the Central Committee demanding freedom of voice. The pasty
academics grumble, list grievances, plot to meet publicly
as the Petőfi Circle. Never before a display of dissatisfaction,
and the people hold their breath, waiting like abused children
for the backhand. But the Party rears up like an elephant surprised
by a mouse, and scared is a look that doesn't fade.

February 15, 1956: A Good Worker

Rajk then Rákosi then Nagy then Rákosi.
Now no more Rákosi? Teachers
whisper, rip pages from our school
books to match today's truth.
Krushchev drinks tea with Tito, denounces
Stalin in a secret speech that isn't secret.
How Daddy spins Mama around the living
room, both of them red in the face
with laughing. I am nauseous
with confusion.
Handbills litter the street urging freedoms
for artists. Haven't they always been free
to proclaim the glory of our nation?
I want to be a good worker, a wife
with many children, but good
today is denounced tomorrow.
Erzsi married a supervisor at the steel factory,
a man of good standing and Party membership,
but Mama says she is as good
as dead, and we didn't make the wedding.
Sunday at Stalin Square, I pointed. Zsuzsi hissed,
slapped my hand down, but too late. Mama followed
my gaze.
Erzsi had a fur muff, held the arm of her new
husband. She walked past us in Stalin's
shadow, pulling her fancy hat low.

June 27, 1956: Peril

Jóska mocks the Petőfi Circle, resenting
unscuffed shoes, smooth palms that never held
a hoe or hammer, but he scampers

to the meetings. Strange to hear demands
in the air, as if the currents they ride on
are free. Remember, comrades, when a discontented

sigh could get you whisked away by the ÁVH?
Those days aren't far behind us, or far ahead.
They've mounted speakers to the walls

for the mob outside. Beneath the calls
for independence, I make out faith
that we'll stand shoulder to shoulder

with soldiers from the West. The cries
stretch past thousands to my ears—bring
Nagy back, return Gerő to Rákosi's lap,

grant freedoms of voice and pen.
I hear another voice pressing against
the din. "Hush, you stupid men; you'll get

us killed," Zsuzsika sputters, old enough
to remember consequences,
smart enough to keep her voice down.

July 18, 1956: All the Rope

The last of the politicals released from jail, the walls of barbed
wire dismantled, border guards sent home. Austria just one step
further across a field, one well-timed bribe away. The resignation
of Rákosi, the toleration of dissent. I know what they think, "Give
these fools enough rope and they'll make a knotted mess of it."
But Hungarians are greedy; seeing coils held loosely in an uncertain
hand, they pull fast.

October 3, 1956: An Odd Alliance

Daddy doesn't know we know he sneaks
  away at night with István. He thumps enough to wake
  the building, and István sings in the hall.
Mama's never mad, just calls us to her bed, not pretending
  she thinks us still asleep.
She sighs and says "stupid asses", pets our hair
  and tells us, "let men be men." We nod, pretending
  to understand though maybe Zsuzsi does and won't say.
István isn't drunk anymore. He dresses sharp in pressed
  brown slacks and a handsome leather cap.
Maybe that is a man being a man.
Zsuzsi says Daddy and István are bad, meeting with outlaws,
  talking about Polish riots.
But Daddy and István are good men, probably talking
  about guns and pork sandwiches, the way good men
  must certainly do.

October 6, 1956: Funeral

Let's not fool ourselves. Rehabilitation in death
won't raise Rajk from Hell on angel wings.
A nation desperate for a sliver of sovereignty, we make

heroes out of home-grown oppressors,
forgetting, in death, their own list of victims.
Three hundred thousand walked behind

the coffin, each person mourning
something in that box other than old
Communist bones. I shuffled along, my eyes

brimming with useless brine, mourning
the man I married. He stayed behind
in Sátoraljaújhely Prison and sent home

a stranger. Today we bury the dead we've clung to,
grasp whatever is at hand to pull ourselves
to standing and learn to cherish what is left.

October 22, 1956: Power Shifts

After fucking half of Europe, the Russians become impotent.
The Poles hold elections, select a leader Krushchev hardly knows
let alone approved, and the Ruszkis stand there holding limp dicks.
Hungary is next. Nagy re-admitted to the Party. Szeged students
resurrect the opposition party, formalize dissent. They meet tonight,
their ranks swelled with workers not so wet behind the ears.
The Party gazes east, their backs turned, waiting for word
from Moscow. Awake, *Magyars*! The time is now.

4. Uprising

A man quite unprepared to die
Is merest riff-raff in my eye,
Thinking ragged life is dearer
Even than this country's honour.
—**Sándor Petőfi, "National Song"**

October 23, 1956: Morning

Where, in this forsaken city, is my
knuckleheaded husband? I can see
the students, thousands of them,

like a mirage across the Danube, marching
down Beloiannisz road. That's just Jóska's
style—a pilgrimage to Bem invoking

solidarity with the Poles. Or is he crouched
at the feet of Petőfi with the workers, ripping
the sickle from the flag as if he never spent

eighteen months in jail? Demands
are flying, spreading like a virus:
democracy, repeal of reparations,

a new government under Nagy. The withdrawal
of Soviet troops—one charge even the broadsheets
won't print. The bear is sleeping, boys.

Even now the informants
are watching, taking pictures,
writing notes.

October 23, 1956: Afternoon

"Go home Ruszkis! Go home Ruszkis!"
Zsuzsi and I shout from the garden, joining
    the voices that burst from every window,
    brick and tree leaf, vibrating the railings
    of our gate.
Lenin, Stalin, Rákosi burn in the streets,
    their pictures massed into piles,
    splintered frames lighting up
    like confused zealots.
Mama pushes us inside, slapping
    our bottoms to make us hurry, shrieking
    about agents and guns.
I *know* this is calamity, but it *feels*
    like no party I've ever been to, bodies
    loose and racing, unguarded faces—
    as if all my life everyone has faked
    happiness and now I'm permitted
    to see the danger it brings.

October 23, 1956: Night

Revolution or civil war? Gerő, Rákosi's pet, spews the usual
Soviet swill on the radio, condemning countrymen as counter-
revolutionaries. What about our turn on the air to reclaim our
brothers? To read the 16 Points. When the station director turns
coward and refuses, the crowd uses bricks and clubs as keys to the
doors. ÁVH guns begin our end, but the Hungarian army, stationed
on the fringes, awake from their eleven-year somnambulance.
They pass guns hand over hand to their brothers. We killed every
last one of those ÁVH bastards. The lucky ones died immediately.
The bodies tossed from windows were broken before they hit
the street.

October 24, 1956: The Coming Storm

I wake in the inky hour of dawn
to rolls of thunder. Remembering
my line of clothes, I pull back

the curtain to assess damage.
No rain, lightning the wrong color
—red and orange crackling like static

between bed sheets being pulled apart. Russia sends
her tanks. The fighting begins once more.
What will come with independence?

Aristocrats reclaiming estates. Workers clinging
to redistributed land. Those men
in the streets, fighting side

by side, stepping over the dying,
do they think they are fighting
for the same thing? Do they believe

they share a future? I gather
blankets, food, the girls and return
to the basement, to '45.

October 24, 1956: Radio Budapest, Home Service, 1:12pm

Women! Do not let your husbands
run into deadly danger. You must prevent them
from supporting counterrevolutionary forces...
Women! Do not let yourself be fooled
by provocateurs.

The bakers have shut off their ovens.
Your daughters have no bread.
Is this the dream for which we cherished

our sleep? Streets battered to rubble, rail lines hacked
to collapsed vertebrae, Budapest's paralyzed spine.
You fool, patriot-drunk and forgetting.

The Red Army is coming, a pestilence
of looters and tanks. They'll laugh
at the destruction they won't need

to wreak, grab at the pickings you've offered up.
Zsuzsika, plump as a tree-ripened peach.
The mobs pollute the air with false anthems,

spreading pride like disease. Are you singing?
Are you ripping the hammer and sickle
from a sooty flag? Has some comrade wrapped

your hands around a rifle? Jóska, the hallway is filled
with ÁVH shouting with loaded tongues, promising
pardons for men who surrender. Their guns are hot

and stinking of sulfur, promising something else.
Tonight I lock the gate and windows.
Strict orders for our safety: keep

the insurgents on the street. Like targets.
You can come home, Jóska,
when you finish your fight.

October 25, 1956: Bloody Thursday

Thousands marched, body to body, to Parliament Square. We
twitched and ached to hear Nagy's first words as the people's Prime
Minister, more evidence of an upturned Rákosi regime. Gerő kicked
out on his ass, replaced by Kádár—one of *us*, a victim of the '51
purges, his balls crushed in a little chat with the ÁVH. The Soviet
soldiers, sick of the fighting, did no more than heckle us from
their tanks. No one knows where the first shot came from,
but the rest followed like hail from clear skies. I ran. Returned
after the crowd scattered, after the sun set in its usual spot behind
the hills as if Hungarians hadn't killed Hungarians. A hundred, two
hundred, bodies slicked the streets with blood—mothers with their
arms splayed across their children as if sleeping. Sometimes a child
alone.

October 26, 1956: The Sound of Revolution

The woman across the street screams
    and screams. Mama put cotton in my ears
    but I still hear.
This morning, four men kicked down her door.
Even I knew she was ÁVH, had fingered
    three men on our street.
The men haven't left and she is still screaming.
Dear God, I am a bad person, to wish
    her already dead.

October 26, 1956: Finally,

we fight for Hungary. We soldiered for the Germans, got shoved
to the front to take Russia's bullets. Those who tried to kill us
claimed themselves liberators, turned our men around to point
guns at themselves. Now soldiers become insurgents, and insurgents
are renamed soldiers. Colonel Maléter assumes command
of the Kilián Barracks and I am eager for battle. Rusted weapons,
jammed triggers, an arsenal of Malatov cocktails and look at us,
driving back the tanks, piling slaughtered Soviets on the sides
of the streets. Finally, something to fight for. Maléter, the man
to lead.

October 27, 1956: The Home Front

Daddy, we heard the cease fire
    on the radio. Why do guns still thunder
    the air? Why have you not
    come home?
Mama took Zsuzsi to find
    food. They came back with bread
    and onion and a piece of dried sausage.
    Even two pears!
The stores are open, though Zsuzsi said
    she walked past bodies to get
    there, one a woman with her shopping
    basket.
Come home, Daddy, before someone's
    daughter must step over your body
    and close her eyes so she doesn't
    see your face.

October 28, 1956: Risking Hope

So Nagy may not have a pants full.
So maybe his communism doesn't suck
on Soviet balls. He announces withdrawal

of Russian troops and shuts down the ÁVH.
But how do we manage a suddenly free
and democratic state? We have no clue

how to rule through methods other than delusion,
bullying, doing what we're told. And Western voices
on the radio have no words, as if all their past

broadcasts encouraging revolt were stories
to soothe us back to sleep each night. Yet one
hope. The U.N. Security Council.

Hungary is on their lips.

October 30, 1956: Taking the Headquarters

I am done. Passed my pistol to a young upstart with fingers itching. With only the backsides of Soviets visible on the streets, our revolution's turned grotesque. The siege was necessary: topple the ÁVH, show them no mercy, show the world we will not stand brutality. So many men still healing from their scars, so many men still broken, so many brothers dead. But it was a massacre of countrymen, bodies with breath left in them burned up and hung in the trees. The last of the resistance is in good hands. I will kill no more Hungarians.

November 1, 1956: An Independent Act

He started small, covertly, digging
up the grave of the Social Democrats, changing
the party name. Zoltán Tildy and Béla Kovács

shake dirt from their cuffs to join
his government. But now Nagy withdraws
us from the Warsaw Pact, and already rumors

spread that more Russian tanks advance
than those leaving. Even a child knows
which Russian pet not to provoke.

Jóska is back, shaken but no bullet holes.
I don't know how much more a man can
take—one hand always reaching for me

while the other clings to a bottle. I've put
the radio away, keep the papers out
of the house, but he won't remain still.

Every '45 party and a dozen new ones
petition for their piece of the coalition
government. Cardinal Mindszenty makes

demands as they unlock his cell door.
Jóska will be sucked into the fray, but I'm telling
you, the Russians won't stand for such boldness.

And the West remains silent—a fat cat
who waited to pounce then fell asleep in its
crouch, too content in its comfort to bother.

November 2, 1956: The Calm Before

Fools, all of us. Yesterday, Kádár proclaimed a glorious uprising.
Today no one can find his trace. Jutka swears he played both sides,
ran to join the Russians. I hope for a kidnapping like in the early
days. Reports arrive from both Eger and Györ: Soviet tanks creep
back in, surround airports, the Ruszkies claiming evacuation
of troops. Radio static can't hide the strain in Nagy's throat,
but the UN is deaf to his plea for support. Fools to trust the West
and their cries of revolution, their promises to finish what we start.
Budapest waits, its streets empty except for women creeping around
the unrecognizable remains of battle, baskets on their arms. In every
home the radio murmurs on and on, announcers now speaking
of Egypt and Israel. So what the hell is the Suez Canal?

November 4, 1956: The Storm

Budapest burns. The ground shakes
   like the world is ending and God must
   punish all those left alive.
The Russian bombs aren't shy this time,
   smashing through walls to seek out
   living rooms and children's beds
   before they explode.
We go back to the cellar, turn white
   with plaster dust that falls with each
   rumble.
Our neighbor, Mrs. Horváth, gives
   me and Zsuzsi suckers to keep
   the dust from our mouths, but
   Zsuzsi says don't eat the Communist's
   candy.
Mama says hush and we suck
   our pops.
Daddy has left again with István
   and a gun. Mr. Horváth
   is out there, too, on the other side,
   and I imagine a big red line down
   Belgrád Pier.
When the Americans come, how will they tell
   us apart?

November 6, 1956: Who has Come, Who is Left

Nagy and his cronies granted refuge
in the Yugoslav Embassy,
Mindszenty in the American one.

Where is asylum for the fighter, his family?
The Westerners have come,
but only to gape and jaw. Journalists

holed up at the Astoria, breaking
for tea time and beer, wandering out
to a building that's just been shelled

to take photos. They leave us
to the Ruszki bombs and soldiers
(their vengeance won't take

prisoners) and drive their convoys
to Vienna where they eat sausage
and buy crystal and talk about their close

calls—the one that dropped
so near it shook the walls. And Jóska
on the street, on his third risked life,

a hero in the story they wire home,
but a man they will forget by the time
they scoot their chairs in to tomorrow's eggs.

November 8: In the Phone Booth

Even a street fight has its tactics, its front lines, its medics
and supply brigade. Weapons in short supply, we stash our arms
in phone booths for the next fighter, a scattered but efficient arsenal.
It was in a phone booth that I understood we will lose—guns piled
to the knees, spilling into the street. There will be heroes. Maybe
legends. Maléter creating an army from a pile of bent and fitful
men. Lázár the painter, bicycling through battles with his brushes
and pots, his steady hand branding each tank and gun barrel
with the Kossuth coat of arms. Tómas, the peg-legged soldier
who was everywhere and never to be found, teaching green
and eager students—rip up cobblestones to slow the tank, toss
a Molotov cocktail in the engine vent. It has been glorious, the false
victory. So many guns in the phone booth, I take two.

November 10, 1956: Accounting

The air is quiet. Daddy is home
    but he is as silent as uprooted
    cobblestones.
Mama screeches at stray
    gunshots, calling Russians ugly
    names, but Daddy says hush,
    hush, hush.
Alive: Mama, Daddy, Zsuzsi,
    Teréz, István. Also the Horváths
    who come and go without
    ducking because they are Communists.
They bring us food and even
    Mama says they are a blessing.
István says Erzsébet is also fine,
    but Mama won't count her.
It's harder to list who got killed.
The dead are being loaded
    into carts, disappearing
    from the streets.

November 12, 1956: The Spoils

It was not for nothing. Hungary seized the world's gaze and we hold it like a staged tragedy. The USSR and that double-crossing Kádár can do nothing without global scrutiny—every free man in the West rooting for the revolutionaries. There will be no retribution.

November 15, 1956: Camera-Ready

Listen to the reports, Jutka. Kádár *endorses* the multi-party system,
workers councils, free elections. His disappearance was crafty,
not treason, lurking behind the scrim of chaos to prepare
negotiations. We will harvest the choice fruit of socialism—medicine
and education for everyone, not just the elite. Get
your head out of your ass, my darling wife. It was not for nothing.

November 17, 1956: Ha

The nurses at Péterfy Street Hospital act
more stunned with each telling, as if they didn't
know their halls were an underground center

of resistance. It begins again—informants
and raids, arrests and disappearances.
We woke the bear and he's shaking

off the lull of a long sleep, his belly rumbling.
The fighting, the deaths, all for nothing.
Jóska hides again. Not even I can know where.

November 21, 1956: Reversal

Kádár's new cooperation with the workers?
A patient ear bent to our demands?
Tell me the Soviet tanks surrounding

the National Sports Hall are there to support
the conference of workers councils.
No one allowed in. Or out. Is the West

watching this? Or have they already turned
away bored, the curtain coming down
on these final, hackneyed acts?

November 22, 1956: Unlikely Angel

The shouting wakes me.
    It comes from outside, but no
    guns or shells or noises of dying.
A yelling man on our curb and I peek
    out the window to see
    a gun turret pointed at my face.
Zsuzsi at the other window,
    another tank.
Mama pulls us to the kitchen but no room
    is safe. Men won't stop banging
    on our door and we wait for it to break.
But Mr. Horváth. We hear him
    march outside, match the yelling man
    curse for curse.
"A sergeant," Mama says.
Mr. Horváth shows his card, some
    papers, waves his arms at our window
    and we duck.
When mama lifts her head again,
    the sergeant and the tanks
    have gone away.

November 23, 1956: Making Plans

Horváth convinced them of nothing
other than Jóska's absence. They'll be
back if they aren't surveilling the house

already. I sent word to Jóska
last night. He must get it. He must
meet us at the house in Sopron.

We leave as if to market—an empty
basket, the girl's school satchels
filled with a day's worth of food

and a few hidden valuables. I meant
to buy a decent coat for Erika. She must
make do. The key to our home heavy

like an anchor in my pocket and no word
to Teréz or István or my whore
sister. To protect them, though

they won't understand.
The gate closes. I tell the girls
don't look back.

November 24, 1956: Retribution

Nagy was tricked, lured from asylum by an outstretched hand,
a meeting with Kádár. Then arrested, then deported. No one is safe.
Jutka sent word. I travel at night through farming villages, dress
like a drunken peasant, rave like I've been separated from my mind.
I almost convince myself. Jutka, you must be close to Sopron.
My clock has stopped once more.

November 25, 1956: Reunion

Daddy comes and stinks like a farm dog.
Still, Mama grabs him as if he were falling
    off the edge of a cliff.
We are hungry but Mama says the cafes
    are closed. She treats me like a baby, and
    I pretend I don't know.
But I know we are hiding. I know Daddy fought
    on the wrong side. I know we are eating
    the last of our salami and bread in the strange
    man's basement.
I know he is not unfriendly, though he twitches
    like a mouse in a cat's mouth.
He will take us over the mountain.
Mama tells us to be brave.
We leave when the moon goes down.

November 25, 1956: The Crossing

The girls are as grim as Jutka, as flint-carved. But who am I
to permit myself hope when so many have been captured or shot or
sliced by shrapnel from a land mine that "does not exist." I feel
nothing, my body numbed by freezing water in this ditch where
we've crouched for an hour. A Soviet patrol almost caught us
in their lights when we crossed the highway. Now their truck paces
relentlessly. Maybe they saw a boot heel or coat hem. Maybe
they wait us out, laughing at our screaming knees, our whimpering
children. The sun rises in six hours.

November 25, 1956: Erzsébet Szilágyi

They're gone. No word, no letter. Thinking
only of themselves. We could have salvaged

their belongings, made enough money to bribe ourselves
into a new flat. Instead, the police dragged

even the girls' shoes away. Teréz's heart is nearly
broken. István drinks himself into a dribbling mess.

And I've been tossed aside like a sock long past
darning. To think I believed that my bitch

sister and her coward husband would
have forgiven, taken me back, taken

me with them when they left. Instead, she used
me like a maid for twelve years and was shocked

when I found love in Jóska's arms. She is lucky
I am done with him. With a snap

of my fingers he'd be back sniffing at my skirts.
Does she not know I married this limp dick

of a man to save her from scandal, to keep
her husband in his place. Everything was

for Jutka. And this isn't finished. I will find
them. I will claim my family and my place.

November 26, 1956: The Other Side of the Mountain

I slide on my bottom half the way
    down, my skirt dragging
    with mud, my stockings itchy
    with gravel and twigs.
The strange man says Austrians will give
    us bread and lard. They will give us tea
    and sit us by a fire.
Everyone walks faster, Daddy chanting
    a marching tune all his own, and I walk
    close to listen.
"Safe now, safe now, we are safe safe now."
Zsuzsi says we will get mittens before we leave.
Then America where want is a wish granted.
What I wish for: new shoes and a garden
    with a cherry tree and lemon
    candies and a fat striped cat.

November 26, 1956: Behind us

the mountain, dawn glinting like its diadem.
Before us a horizon, a village in the distance,
the strangers we will ask for help.

Behind us my country,
my herb plants on the window sill,
my mother's silver vase, Zsuzsi's

ribbons lost beneath the dresser, Erika's
dirty spoons of snuck jam. Jóska's
silence doesn't scare me. It is a strong

man's quiet, his reserves welling
inside him. We walk and the village
becomes alive, smoke rising from

chimneys, the outline of roofs. Behind
us, Hungary shrivels, its landscapes
blurring, faces already beginning

to fade.

At the end of the Hungarian Revolution, 2,740 Hungarian citizens were dead. Approximately 250,000 fled the country. Between 1956 and 1958, the Kádár regime reprisals led to over 25,000 arrests, 1,300 imprisonments and 2,000 executions, including Imre Nagy, Pal Maléter, and other leaders of the revolution. The government lost credibility and the country lost many of its most competent and talented citizens.

Sources

Bideleaux, Robert and Ian Jeffries. *A History of Eastern Europe: Crisis and Change*. New York: Routledge, 1998.

Dent, Bob. *Budapest 1956: Locations of Drama*. Budapest: Európa Könyvkiadó, 2006.

Evaluation Information Items. Hungarian Unit. Records of Radio Free Europe/Radio Liberty Research Institute (RFE/RL RI). HU OSA 300-40-4, containers 1–6. Budapest: Open Society Archives, October 2006.

Kalman, Bobbie and Barbara Bedell. *Refugee Child: My Memories of the 1956 Hungarian Revolution*. New York: Crabtree Publishing Co, 2006.

Katin, Miriam. *We are on Our Own*. Montreal, Drawn & Quarterly, 2006.

Kontler, László. *A History of Hungary*. New York: Palgrave McMillan, 2002.

Korda, Michael. *Journey to a Revolution*. New York: HarperCollins, 1996.

Lasky, Melvin J., comp and ed. *The Hungarian revolution: A white book. The story of the October uprising as recorded in documents, dispatches, eye-witness accounts, and world-wide reactions*. New York: F.A. Praeger, 1957.

Lessing, Erich. *Revolution in Hungary: The 1956 Budapest Uprising*. London: Thames & Hudson, 2006.

Lettis, Richard and William I. Morris, eds. *The Hungarian Revolt, October 23–November 4, 1956*. Simon Publications, 2001. http://www.hungarianhistory.com/lib/revolt/revo4.htm.

Litván, György, János M. Bak, and Lyman Howard Legters. *The Hungarian Revolution of 1956: Reform, Revolt and Repression 1953–1963*. New York: Longman Publishing Group, 1996.

Lomax, Bill. *Hungary 1956*. London: Allison & Busby Limited, 1976.

Márai, Sándor. *Memoir of Hungary: 1944–1948*. Budapest: Corvina Books; Central European University Press, 1996.

March, Michael, ed. *Descriptions of a Struggle: The Picador Book of Cotemporary East European Prose*. London: Picador, 1995.

Petőfi, Sándor. "National Song." Trans. Alan Dixon. *Visegrad Magic Cube*. Web.

Notes

1   Gyula Háy, a Hungarian poet, wrote this in a essay for the prominent journal *Irodalmi Újság* (*Literary Gazette*) in the summer of 1956. He went to jail for six years for his words.

5   Translation of Sándor Petőfi's "National Song" by Alan Dixon.

12   Of the estimated 600,000 Hungarian men that were deported to labor camps in Siberia, 200,000 were civilians, and 200,000 perished there.

13   Kecskemét, a town west of Budapest, was home to many *pusztas*, or farming estates.

The *pengő* was Hungary's currency from 1927 to 1946. After the end of the war, the *pengő* suffered the highest rate of hyperinflation ever recorded, and when the government couldn't get the inflation under control, they replaced it with the *forint*.

15   At the Allies' insistence, the Soviets authorized the only essentially free election in Eastern Europe in November 1945 in Hungary. At the time, there were several political parties vying for seats in the coalition government.

The Independent Smallholder Party was the Hungarian Communist Party's main political rival.

Pálinka is a double-distilled brandy made from fruit, most often apricots, peaches, plums, or pears.

16   Imre Nagy, Minister of Agriculture, redistributed the aristocracy's land among the peasant population.

17   The *forint* was the currency of the Austro-Hungarian Empire from 1862–1892. It was re-introduced in Hungary in 1946 after the inflation of the *pengő* spiraled out of control. It is the current currency of Hungary.

18   On February 10, 1947, representatives from 21 nations signed the Treaty of Paris, which required that Hungary pay the Soviet Union exorbitant war reparations. Despite the fact that the treaty allowed Hungary to re-assume its status as a sovereign state, it also decreed the Soviets to be the sole occupying force in Hungary (on the premise that they needed to secure trade routes from the USSR to Austria).

19   Ferenc Nagy and Béla Kóvacs were leaders of the Smallholder Party, which in 1947 had the majority seats in a coalition government that the Soviet Union agreed to support.

21   As part of the 1947 Paris Peace Treaty, Hungary was forced to pay the Soviet Union $200,000,000 in reparations and another $100,000,000 to Czechoslovakia and Yugoslavia.

22   *Szabad Nép* was the mouthpiece of the Hungarian Working Peoples (i.e. Communist) Party (HWPP) and became the only legal newspaper in Hungary.

Formerly called the Allamvedélmi Osztály (or State Protection Department), the Államvédelmi Hatóság (ÁVH) translates to the State Protection Authority. The ÁVH was the HWPP's secret police controlled by Soviet advisors.

23   Cardinal József Mindszenty was head of the Roman Catholic Church in Hungary. Because he was vocal about his opposition to communism and Stalinist persecution, he was arrested, jailed, tortured, show-tried and sentenced to life in prison.

26   Imre Nagy, the popular Minister of Agriculture who redistributed land after the war, opposed the Soviet Politburo's plan for agricultural collectivization. He was deemed "counterrevolutionary" and, though allowed to maintain his position, he was ostracized by the Central Committee and became powerless. László Rajk served as Minister of the Interior (during which time he organized and ran the ÁVH) and the Minister of Foreign Affairs. He was a political threat to Mátyás Rákosi (who was the

Soviet-backed power broker of the HWPP), so Rákosi accused Rajk of false charges.

Mátyás Rákosi was the *de facto* dictator of Hungary between 1945 and 1956. While he never served as prime minister, he pulled all the strings as the General Secretary of the HWPP. He, himself, was a puppet and disciple of Stalin.

27 Thousands of individuals living in Budapest were forced from their homes, deported to the most rural areas of the country, and forced to work on collective farms (*kolkhozek*) for very little pay. Their apartments and belongings were seized by the HWPP, which were then often redistributed to high-ranking Party members.

29 The HWPP created a "peace loan" subscription service to build up the country's military strength. Hungarians were asked to voluntarily contribute to the loan. Like all "voluntary" Communist initiatives, the consequences for not contributing were dire. A person who refused to contribute was considered an enemy of the people, which was a danger to the state. Depending on how "dangerous" the enemy of the people was, he or she could be sent to a work camp, a *kolkosz,* or jail.

31 The stories in this section come from interviews conducted by Radio Free Europe with Hungarian refugees who fled the country. Transcriptions of the interviews were accessed at the Open Society Archives in Budapest (see bibliography). In most cases, names have been changed.

35 The Arrow Cross party, Hungary's pro-Nazi socialist party, came into power at the end of WWII. During its brief reign, the party murdered ten to fifteen thousand Jews and deported another 80,000 to Auschwitz.

The Jewish ghetto of Budapest was formed in June, 1944. Within a few weeks, approximately 200,000 Jews moved into 2,000 homes.

45 A *puszta* is a remote farm surrounded by fields, often part of an aristocratic estate.

55 All parents were pressured to enroll their children in the Young Pioneers, a Communist youth group structured similarly to the Scouts, except its main purpose was Communist indoctrination. Children were encouraged to report their parents if they caught their parents saying or doing anything that suggested they were an enemy of the people, including reading Western literature, voicing discontent about the government or communism, buying black market items, or saying anything uncomplimentary about Communist officials.

59 Hungarian Communists were divided into two factions—those who were homegrown and remained underground in Hungary before and during World War II (this Communist "cell" was led by László Rajk) and those who spent time in the Soviet Union between the two World Wars (the "Muscovites" led by Mátyás Rákosi). After the Soviet Army invaded Hungary in 1944, the underground Communists emerged and the Muscovites returned home. Soon, the Muscovites, who were favored by the Soviets (particularly Stalin), muscled the homegrown Communists out of any position of power. Once Stalin died, however, the Muscovite advantage became shaky.

Stakhanovite—A model worker who regularly surpassed production quotas; a kiss-ass.

60 At the end of WWII, many Arrow Cross members changed their pro-Germany Nazi affiliation to a pro-Soviet Communist affiliation. Many Arrow Crossers were the first ones in line to apply for a Communist Party card.

62 Imre Nagy, the popular Minister of Agriculture who redistributed land after the war, was Prime Minister from 1953–1955. After Stalin's death, Nagy attempted a more liberal socialism with his "New Course," but the Soviet Politboro was displeased with the direction he was taking and sacked him in April, 1955.

63 Nagy's reforms refer to his "New Course."
   Tokaji is a sweet wine from the region of Tokaj-Hegyalja with a long national history. Only wines from this region can be labeled *Tokaji*, and *Tokaji* is mentioned in the official Hungarian national anthem.

67 The Petőfi Circle, named after Sander Petőfi, the famous national poet who had fought for Hungarian freedom in 1848 against the Austrian Empire, was formed by writers, academics and intellectuals in April 1955. They met regularly and semi-openly in hopes of changing Communist practices. The group was soon overwhelmed by thousands who came to voice discontent.

68 Rákosi was ousted as General Secretary of the HWPP under pressure from the Soviet Politburo in June 1956. The reasons were many: growing public dissatisfaction with the Hungarian economy; material shortages and escalating foreign debt; demands for change; and Khrushchev's condemnation of Stalin and many of Stalin's practices, including his cult of personality (Rákosi was closely tied to Stalin). Rákosi was replaced by Ernő Gerő and was forced by the Soviets to move to the Soviet Union and abandon Hungarian politics.
   Stalin's Square, now called Hero's Square, contained a towering stature of Stalin.

69 See note above. Ernő Gerő was widely considered to be Rákosi's puppet.

71 In June of '56, the Polish people started a series of massive protests against the Communist government demanding better working conditions. Despite the violent repression they incurred, the Poznań 1956 protests (as they were called for taking part at the Poznań's Cegielski Factories) led to a decrease in Soviet control of their government in October. These events were a source of inspiration for the Hungarian people.

72 At one of the first Petőfi Circle meetings, László Rajk's widow, Julia, protested the accusations against her husband, and, after

many protestations and pressure from the Soviets, who were reconciling with Tito (Rajk was accused of Titoist sympathies), the Hungarian government rehabilitated Rajk. This meant that they retracted the accusations against him and restored his reputation. On October 6, several hundred thousand mourners joined the processional that moved Rajk's remains from its secret burial place in the woods to the Pantheon of the Heroes of the Labor Movement.

73 On October 16, 1956, university students in Szeged thumbed their noses at the official Communist student union, the DISZ, by re-establishing the MEFESZ (Union of Hungarian University and Academy Students), a democratic student organization previously banned under the Rákosi dictatorship.

77 József Bem was a Polish and Hungarian war hero who fought for both Polish independence (in the 1830 Uprising) and Hungarian independence (in the 1848 War of Independence). A statue of Bem stands next to the Danube on the Buda side of Budapest.

Students at the Technical University in Budapest put together the "16 Point Manifesto" stating demands of the government for reform. The demands were widely printed and distributed. There is some debate as to whether the original manifesto included other demands (such as the removal of Soviet troops) that were considered too risky and were cut.

78 See note above.

81 The quoted text is from a transcription of a Radio Budapest Home Service broadcast. A complete transcription of radio broadcasts in Hungary from October 23 to November 4, 1956 can be found in the book *The Hungarian Revolt, October 23–November 4, 1956* on the Historical Text Archive website (see Sources).

Because the HWPP deemed its agenda revolutionary, they considered those participating in the uprising to be "counterrevolutionaries."

83 As a result of his prior efforts at reform when he was Prime Minister in 1953, Imre Nagy became the figurehead of the popular uprising that started on October 23, and the people demanded that he be appointed Prime Minister again. The Soviet Politburo, in seeming attempts to avoid an escalation, appointed Nagy as Prime Minister, and thousands marched to the Parliament building on October 24th to hear Nagy speak.

    János Kádár was the first secretary of the Hungarian Communist Party (HWPP) between 1943–1945. Under the Rákosi regime, Kádár was arrested, tortured, sentenced to life imprisonment and kicked out of the Party, primarily because he was a "home-grown" Communist. The purges mentioned here refer to the purges of the Communist Party at the beginning of the Rakosi regime when hundreds of home-grown Communists suffered the same fate as Kádár. Like Kádár, many of them were released from prison and rehabilitated in '53 and '54 after Stalin's death.

    It is generally believed that the first shots came from the roof of the nearby Agricultural building, and that the shooters were members of the ÁVH.

85 Pál Maléter fought on the Eastern Front in WWII, until captured by the Red Army. He became a Communist, trained in sabotage and was sent back to Hungary. In 1956 he was Colonel in the Hungarian Army and a commander of an armored division stationed in Budapest. He was sent to suppress the rebellion, but on making contact with the insurgents, he decided to join them, taking charge of the Kilian Barracks which the insurgents made their headquarters. He was the most prominent member of the Hungarian military to change sides. He was also, in this writer's opinion, fabulously handsome.

87 On October 28, The UN Security Council met in an emergency session to consider Soviet intervention in the Hungarian uprising. It was generally agreed, however, that no action would get

past the Soviet power of veto. Still, Western forces tried to get the matter in front of the United Nations.

88 On October 30, on hearing rumors that the ÁVH were holding prisoners at the HWPP headquarters, armed protestors attacked the building. Over 20 ÁVH officers were killed, some of them lynched by the mob. Hungarian army tanks sent to rescue the Party headquarters mistakenly bombarded the building. Revolutionary leaders in Hungary condemned the incident, and the mob violence soon died down.

89 Upon Nagy's reinstatement to power, he changed the name of the HWPP to the Hungarian Socialist Workers Party (HSWP). He also re-instituted a multi-party system, and many leaders of the pre-1948 political parties petitioned to join the coalition. Tildy and Kovács were ousted as leaders of the Socialist Democrats before the Party was subsumed by the Hungarian Communist Party to form the HWPP.

The Soviet government tolerated Nagy's reinstatement and his move toward multi-party rule. However, his attempt to withdraw Hungary from the Warsaw Pact and his appeal, through the UN, to the western powers to recognize Hungary as a neutral state crossed the line, and the Soviets began the process of sending in more troops to suppress the uprising. Some suggest that the Soviets were already planning to reestablish control, and Nagy's withdrawal from the Warsaw Pact was a good excuse to re-invade.

90 On October 25, Kádár was elected Secretary-General of the HSWP. He was also Minister of State of the Nagy Cabinet.

In July of 1956, Egypt nationalized the Suez Canal, an important conduit of oil, after the U.S. and Great Britain withdrew funding in response to Egypt's increasingly cozy relations with the USSR. The nationalization compromised British and French economic interests, and working in partnership with Israel, they decided to intervene in October. Britain deliberately neglected to inform the American government, believing that Egypt's engagement with Communist states would persuade the Americans to support their actions. The U.S. government, however, fearing an escalation of tensions with the USSR, didn't support the invasion. Many believe that the Suez Crisis not only diverted U.S. attention away from the Soviet interference in the Hungarian uprising, but it also further discouraged the U.S. from supporting the Hungarian Freedom Fighters in order to avoid military engagement with the USSR.

92 The Soviets re-entered the city on November 4th, and, after making a final radio plea to the U.S. and the rest of the world for help and support, Nagy and a few of his cabinet members (excluding Kádár) took refuge in the Yugoslav Embassy.

The Astoria is a famous Budapest hotel built in 1914.

93 The Kossuth Coat of Arms was first adopted during the 1848 Hungarian Revolution and War of Independence against the Hapsburg Empire. The shield was named after Lajos Kossuth, the President-Regent of Hungary at the time. During the '56 Revolution, the Freedom Fighters once again adopted the Kossuth Coat of Arms.

95 On November 1, the day that Kádár disappeared from public view in Hungary, he traveled to Moscow with help from the Soviet Embassy in Budapest. The Soviets told him that he must help put an end to the Hungarian "counter-revolution." He initially resisted and agreed only when the Soviet leaders told him that military action was already underway, and that if he didn't want to become the new Prime Minister that they would reinstate the old regime. When the Soviet tanks moved into Budapest on November 4, Kádár was already at work creating the "Revolutionary Worker-Peasant Government."

98 Kádár initially stated that he was willing to work with Hungary's workers' councils which, during the Revolution, revoked unreasonable regulations and worked to create an economy that pro-

tected the workers' interests. However, on November 21, Soviet forces prevented a national convention of workers' councils, and the Kádár government instituted a general ban on their meeting.

101 Sopron is a Hungarian town near the Austrian Border.

Kádár offered to meet with Nagy and other leaders of the Revolution, promising them that if they came to the meeting, no harm would come to them. When Nagy and the others left the asylum of the Yugoslav Embassy for the meeting, they were arrested by Soviet forces. A similar, though earlier, fate befell Pál Maléter. On November 4th, at a meeting with Soviet military forces in a town near Budapest, the Soviets arrested and imprisoned him, defying international law prohibiting such acts.

Acknowledgments

I am grateful to the following magazines and journals which first published, sometimes in slightly altered forms, the following poems:

CALYX—Learning the Dead Language
HEArt; Human Equity Through Art—Jóska, August 23, 1952:
    The Political Prisoner
Midway Journal—March 14, 1945: Injury
Poem—November 29, 1944: The Russians are marching;
    March 3, 1945: Outlaw Dreams of Budapest
Poetry International—December 14, 1952: In the Cupboard

Special thanks to: the Jerome Foundation for a Travel and Study Grant, which enabled me to travel to Budapest and to conduct the necessary research for this book; the Blue Mountain Center for the time during which much of this book was reconceived and drafted; the Open Society Archives at Central European University and the Institute for the Research of the 1956 Revolution, which opened their collections to me; archivists Botond Barta, Robert Parnica, and András Mink and librarian Andrea Boros for their assistance and camaraderie; and Dr. László Kontler and Dr. Tibor Frank for their interviews. Thanks also to Rachel Ambrose, Dániel Dányi, Matt Ellis, Gábor Gyukics, Betti Haasz, Aaron Hunter, Ryan James, Simon Milton, Réka Sáfrány, and Andrew Singer for their friendship, guidance and encouragement as I negotiated their beautiful city. Aaron Angello's, Joelle Biele's and Molly Sutton Kiefer's feedback on this book was invaluable. Finally, my deepest gratitude to Floyd Gabriel, who said the story should be written and that I was the one to write it.

Photo: D. Graham Holmes

Michele Battiste's first full-length collection, *Ink for an Odd Cartography*, was a finalist for the St. Lawrence Book Award and was published by Black Lawrence Press in 2009. She was a finalist for the 2013 National Poetry Series and is the author of four chapbooks, the most recent of which is *Lineage* (Binge Press, 2012). She received a Jerome Foundation Travel and Study Grant to conduct research in Budapest for *Uprising*. In 2007, she was awarded a Blue Mountain Center Residency to complete the first draft. Michele has taught poetry writing for Wichita State University (WSU), the Prison Arts Program in Hutchinson, KS, Gotham Writers' Workshops, and the national writing program Teen Ink. She lives in Colorado where she raises funds for organizations undoing corporate evil.